HAL•LEONARD

JAZZ PLAY-ALONG®

Book and CD for B♭, E♭, C and Bass Clef Instruments

Volume 167

JOHNNY MANDEL

T0085619

Arranged by Mark Taylor

Produced by Jim Roberts, Craig Fraedrich, and Paul Murtha

BOOK

CD

ISBN 978-1-4768-2122-1

HAL•LEONARD®
CORPORATION

7777 W. BLUEMOUND RD. P.O. BOX 13819 MILWAUKEE, WI 53213

Visit Hal Leonard Online at
www.halleonard.com

JOHNNY MANDEL

Volume 167

Arranged by Mark Taylor
Produced by Jim Roberts, Craig Fraedrich, and Paul Murtha

Featured Players:

Graham Breedlove–Trumpet
John Desalme–Tenor Sax and Clarinet
Tony Nalker–Piano
Jim Roberts–Guitar
Paul Henry–Bass
Todd Harrison–Drums

Recorded at Bias Studios, Springfield, Virginia
Bob Dawson, Engineer

HOW TO USE THE CD:

Each song has <u>two</u> tracks:

1) Split Track/Melody

Woodwind, Brass, Keyboard, and **Mallet Players** can use this track as a learning tool for melody style and inflection.

Bass Players can learn and perform with this track – remove the recorded bass track by turning down the volume on the LEFT channel.

Keyboard and **Guitar Players** can learn and perform with this track – remove the recorded piano part by turning down the volume on the RIGHT channel.

2) Full Stereo Track

Soloists or **Groups** can learn and perform with this accompaniment track with the RHYTHM SECTION only.

CD
🔹13: SPLIT TRACK/MELODY
🔹14: FULL STEREO TRACK

SONG FROM M*A*S*H
(SUICIDE IS PAINLESS)

WORDS AND MUSIC BY MIKE ALTMAN
AND JOHNNY MANDEL

C VERSION

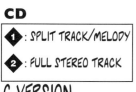

CINNAMON AND CLOVE

WORDS AND MUSIC BY MARILYN BERGMAN,
ALAN BERGMAN AND JOHN MANDEL

C VERSION

CLOSE ENOUGH FOR LOVE

CD
3: SPLIT TRACK/MELODY
4: FULL STEREO TRACK

C VERSION

MUSIC BY JOHNNY MANDEL
WORDS BY PAUL WILLIAMS

EMILY

FROM THE MGM MOTION PICTURE THE AMERICANIZATION OF EMILY

MUSIC BY JOHNNY MANDEL
WORDS BY JOHNNY MERCER

C VERSION

CD
◆ **7** : SPLIT TRACK/MELODY
◆ **8** : FULL STEREO TRACK

NOT REALLY THE BLUES

BY JOHNNY MANDEL

C VERSION

THE SHADOW OF YOUR SMILE
LOVE THEME FROM THE SANDPIPER

MUSIC BY JOHNNY MANDEL
WORDS BY PAUL FRANCIS WEBSTER

THE SHINING SEA

MUSIC BY JOHNNY MANDEL
WORDS BY PEGGY LEE

A Time for Love
From An American Dream

MUSIC BY JOHNNY MANDEL
WORDS BY PAUL FRANCIS WEBSTER

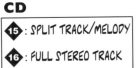

CD
⬦15: SPLIT TRACK/MELODY
⬦16: FULL STEREO TRACK

C VERSION

WHERE DO YOU START?

MUSIC BY JOHNNY MANDEL
WORDS AND MUSIC BY ALAN AND MARILYN BERGMAN

CD
- ◆17 : SPLIT TRACK/MELODY
- ◆18 : FULL STEREO TRACK

C VERSION

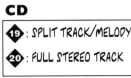

YOU ARE THERE

MUSIC BY JOHNNY MANDEL
WORDS BY DAVE FRISHBERG

C VERSION

SONG FROM M*A*S*H
(SUICIDE IS PAINLESS)

WORDS AND MUSIC BY MIKE ALTMAN
AND JOHNNY MANDEL

CINNAMON AND CLOVE

WORDS AND MUSIC BY MARILYN BERGMAN,
ALAN BERGMAN AND JOHN MANDEL

Bb VERSION

CD

3 : SPLIT TRACK/MELODY
4 : FULL STEREO TRACK

CLOSE ENOUGH FOR LOVE

MUSIC BY JOHNNY MANDEL
WORDS BY PAUL WILLIAMS

Bb VERSION

EMILY

FROM THE MGM MOTION PICTURE THE AMERICANIZATION OF EMILY

MUSIC BY JOHNNY MANDEL
WORDS BY JOHNNY MERCER

Bb VERSION

SOLOS (2 CHORUSES)

NOT REALLY THE BLUES

By Johnny Mandel

Bb VERSION

En la esquina superior derecha: 33

CD
9 : SPLIT TRACK/MELODY
10 : FULL STEREO TRACK

Bb VERSION

THE SHADOW OF YOUR SMILE
LOVE THEME FROM THE SANDPIPER

MUSIC BY JOHNNY MANDEL
WORDS BY PAUL FRANCIS WEBSTER

THE SHINING SEA

MUSIC BY JOHNNY MANDEL
WORDS BY PEGGY LEE

CD

11: SPLIT TRACK/MELODY
12: FULL STEREO TRACK

Bb VERSION

MEDIUM SLOW BOSSA

A TIME FOR LOVE
FROM AN AMERICAN DREAM

MUSIC BY JOHNNY MANDEL
WORDS BY PAUL FRANCIS WEBSTER

Bb VERSION

SLOW BALLAD

WHERE DO YOU START?

MUSIC BY JOHNNY MANDEL
WORDS AND MUSIC BY ALAN AND MARILYN BERGMAN

CD
17 : SPLIT TRACK/MELODY
18 : FULL STEREO TRACK

Bb VERSION

YOU ARE THERE

MUSIC BY JOHNNY MANDEL
WORDS BY DAVE FRISHBERG

: SPLIT TRACK/MELODY
: FULL STEREO TRACK

B♭ VERSION

SONG FROM M*A*S*H
(SUICIDE IS PAINLESS)

WORDS AND MUSIC BY MIKE ALTMAN
AND JOHNNY MANDEL

Eb VERSION

CINNAMON AND CLOVE

WORDS AND MUSIC BY MARILYN BERGMAN,
ALAN BERGMAN AND JOHN MANDEL

Eb VERSION

CLOSE ENOUGH FOR LOVE

MUSIC BY JOHNNY MANDEL
WORDS BY PAUL WILLIAMS

CD
3 : SPLIT TRACK/MELODY
4 : FULL STEREO TRACK

Eb VERSION

EMILY

FROM THE MGM MOTION PICTURE THE AMERICANIZATION OF EMILY

MUSIC BY JOHNNY MANDEL
WORDS BY JOHNNY MERCER

Eb VERSION

NOT REALLY THE BLUES

7 : SPLIT TRACK/MELODY
8 : FULL STEREO TRACK

BY JOHNNY MANDEL

Eb VERSION

THE SHADOW OF YOUR SMILE
LOVE THEME FROM THE SANDPIPER

MUSIC BY JOHNNY MANDEL
WORDS BY PAUL FRANCIS WEBSTER

Eb VERSION

THE SHINING SEA

MUSIC BY JOHNNY MANDEL
WORDS BY PEGGY LEE

CD

⑪ : SPLIT TRACK/MELODY
⑫ : FULL STEREO TRACK

Eb VERSION

A TIME FOR LOVE
FROM AN AMERICAN DREAM

MUSIC BY JOHNNY MANDEL
WORDS BY PAUL FRANCIS WEBSTER

Eb VERSION

CD
🔶17 : SPLIT TRACK/MELODY
🔶18 : FULL STEREO TRACK

WHERE DO YOU START?

MUSIC BY JOHNNY MANDEL
WORDS AND MUSIC BY ALAN AND MARILYN BERGMAN

Eb VERSION

YOU ARE THERE

**MUSIC BY JOHNNY MANDEL
WORDS BY DAVE FRISHBERG**

Eb VERSION

SONG FROM M*A*S*H
(SUICIDE IS PAINLESS)

WORDS AND MUSIC BY MIKE ALTMAN
AND JOHNNY MANDEL

CINNAMON AND CLOVE

WORDS AND MUSIC BY MARILYN BERGMAN,
ALAN BERGMAN AND JOHN MANDEL

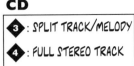

CLOSE ENOUGH FOR LOVE

MUSIC BY JOHNNY MANDEL
WORDS BY PAUL WILLIAMS

EMILY
FROM THE MGM MOTION PICTURE THE AMERICANIZATION OF EMILY

MUSIC BY JOHNNY MANDEL
WORDS BY JOHNNY MERCER

𝄢: C VERSION

SOLOS (2 CHORUSES)

CD

⑦ : SPLIT TRACK/MELODY
⑧ : FULL STEREO TRACK

𝄢 : C VERSION

NOT REALLY THE BLUES

BY JOHNNY MANDEL

THE SHADOW OF YOUR SMILE
LOVE THEME FROM THE SANDPIPER

MUSIC BY JOHNNY MANDEL
WORDS BY PAUL FRANCIS WEBSTER

CD
- ♦ 9 : SPLIT TRACK/MELODY
- ♦ 10 : FULL STEREO TRACK

C VERSION

THE SHINING SEA

MUSIC BY JOHNNY MANDEL
WORDS BY PEGGY LEE

CD
🔢 11 : SPLIT TRACK/MELODY
🔢 12 : FULL STEREO TRACK

𝄢: C VERSION

MEDIUM SLOW BOSSA

A TIME FOR LOVE
FROM AN AMERICAN DREAM

MUSIC BY JOHNNY MANDEL
WORDS BY PAUL FRANCIS WEBSTER

C VERSION

WHERE DO YOU START?

MUSIC BY JOHNNY MANDEL
WORDS AND MUSIC BY ALAN AND MARILYN BERGMAN

CD
17: SPLIT TRACK/MELODY
18: FULL STEREO TRACK

𝄢: C VERSION

SLOW BALLAD

YOU ARE THERE

MUSIC BY JOHNNY MANDEL
WORDS BY DAVE FRISHBERG

Presenting the Hal Leonard JAZZ PLAY-ALONG® SERIES

For use with all B-flat, E-flat, Bass Clef and C instruments, the Jazz Play-Along® Series is the ultimate learning tool for all jazz musicians. With musician-friendly lead sheets, melody cues, and other split-track choices on the included CD, these first-of-a-kind packages help you master improvisation while playing some of the greatest tunes of all time. FOR STUDY, each tune includes a split track with: melody cue with proper style and inflection • professional rhythm tracks • choruses for soloing • removable bass part • removable piano part. FOR PERFORMANCE, each tune also has: an additional full stereo accompaniment track (no melody) • additional choruses for soloing.

Prices, contents, and availability subject to change without notice.

HAL•LEONARD®
CORPORATION
7777 W. BLUEMOUND RD. P.O. BOX 13819
MILWAUKEE, WISCONSIN 53213

For complete songlists and more,
visit Hal Leonard online at
www.halleonard.com

*These CDs do not include split tracks.

1013

Jazz Instruction & Improvisation

BOOKS FOR ALL INSTRUMENTS FROM HAL LEONARD

AN APPROACH TO JAZZ IMPROVISATION
by Dave Pozzi
Musicians Institute Press
Explore the styles of Charlie Parker, Sonny Rollins, Bud Powell and others with this comprehensive guide to jazz improvisation. Covers: scale choices • chord analysis • phrasing • melodies • harmonic progressions • more.
00695135 Book/CD Pack........................$17.95

THE ART OF MODULATING
FOR PIANISTS AND JAZZ MUSICIANS
by Carlos Salzedo &
Lucile Lawrence
Schirmer
The Art of Modulating is a treatise originally intended for the harp, but this edition has been edited for use by intermediate keyboardists and other musicians who have an understanding of basic music theory. In its pages you will find: table of intervals; modulation rules; modulation formulas; examples of modulation; extensions and cadences; ten fragments of dances; five characteristic pieces; and more.
50490581 ....$19.99

BUILDING A JAZZ VOCABULARY
By Mike Steinel
A valuable resource for learning the basics of jazz from Mike Steinel of the University of North Texas. It covers: the basics of jazz • how to build effective solos • a comprehensive practice routine • and a jazz vocabulary of the masters.
00849911 ....$19.95

THE CYCLE OF FIFTHS
by Emile and Laura De Cosmo
This essential instruction book provides more than 450 exercises, including hundreds of melodic and rhythmic ideas. The book is designed to help improvisors master the cycle of fifths, one of the primary progressions in music. Guaranteed to refine technique, enhance improvisational fluency, and improve sight-reading!
00311114 ....$16.99

THE DIATONIC CYCLE
by Emile and Laura De Cosmo
Renowned jazz educators Emile and Laura De Cosmo provide more than 300 exercises to help improvisors tackle one of music's most common progressions: the diatonic cycle. This book is guaranteed to refine technique, enhance improvisational fluency, and improve sight-reading!
00311115 ....$16.95

EAR TRAINING
by Keith Wyatt,
Carl Schroeder and Joe Elliott
Musicians Institute Press
Covers: basic pitch matching • singing major and minor scales • identifying intervals • transcribing melodies and rhythm • identifying chords and progressions • seventh chords and the blues • modal interchange, chromaticism, modulation • and more.
00695198 Book/2-CD Pack $24.95

EXERCISES AND ETUDES FOR THE JAZZ INSTRUMENTALIST
by J.J. Johnson
Designed as study material and playable by any instrument, these pieces run the gamut of the jazz experience, featuring common and uncommon time signatures and keys, and styles from ballads to funk. They are progressively graded so that both beginners and professionals will be challenged by the demands of this wonderful music.
00842018 Bass Clef Edition $16.95
00842042 Treble Clef Edition $16.95

JAZZOLOGY
THE ENCYCLOPEDIA OF JAZZ THEORY FOR ALL MUSICIANS
by Robert Rawlins and
Nor Eddine Bahha
This comprehensive resource covers a variety of jazz topics, for beginners and pros of any instrument. The book serves as an encyclopedia for reference, a thorough methodology for the student, and a workbook for the classroom.
00311167 ....$19.99

JAZZ THEORY RESOURCES
by Bert Ligon
Houston Publishing, Inc.
This is a jazz theory text in two volumes. **Volume 1 includes**: review of basic theory • rhythm in jazz performance • triadic generalization • diatonic harmonic progressions and analysis • substitutions and turnarounds • and more. **Volume 2 includes**: modes and modal frameworks • quartal harmony • extended tertian structures and triadic superimposition • pentatonic applications • coloring "outside" the lines and beyond • and more.
00030458 Volume 1 ....$39.95
00030459 Volume 2 ....$29.95

JOY OF IMPROV
by Dave Frank
and John Amaral
This book/CD course on improvisation for all instruments and all styles will help players develop monster musical skills! Book One imparts a solid basis in technique, rhythm, chord theory, ear training and improv concepts. **Book Two** explores more advanced chord voicings, chord arranging techniques and more challenging blues and melodic lines. The CD can be used as a listening and play-along tool.
00220005 Book 1 – Book/CD Pack......................$27.99
00220006 Book 2 – Book/CD Pack......................$26.99

THE PATH TO JAZZ IMPROVISATION
by Emile and Laura De Cosmo
This fascinating jazz instruction book offers an innovative, scholarly approach to the art of improvisation. It includes in-depth analysis and lessons about: cycle of fifths • diatonic cycle • overtone series • pentatonic scale • harmonic and melodic minor scale • polytonal order of keys • blues and bebop scales • modes • and more.
00310904 ....$14.99

THE SOURCE
THE DICTIONARY OF CONTEMPORARY AND TRADITIONAL SCALES
by Steve Barta
This book serves as an informative guide for people who are looking for good, solid information regarding scales, chords, and how they work together. It provides right and left hand fingerings for scales, chords, and complete inversions. Includes over 20 different scales, each written in all 12 keys.
00240885 ....$18.99

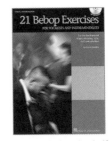

21 BEBOP EXERCISES
by Steve Rawlins
This book/CD pack is both a warm-up collection and a manual for bebop phrasing. Its tasty and sophisticated exercises will help you develop your proficiency with jazz interpretation. It concentrates on practice in all twelve keys — moving higher by half-step — to help develop dexterity and range. The companion CD includes all of the exercises in 12 keys.
00315341 Book/CD Pack....................................$17.95

HAL•LEONARD® CORPORATION
7777 W. BLUEMOUND RD. P.O. BOX 13819 MILWAUKEE, WI 53213

Visit Hal Leonard online at
www.halleonard.com

Prices, contents & availability subject to change without notice.

0113

ARTIST TRANSCRIPTIONS

Artist Transcriptions are authentic, note-for-note transcriptions of today's hottest artists in jazz, pop and rock. These outstanding, accurate arrangements are in an easy-to-read format which includes all essential lines. Artist Transcriptions can be used to perform, sequence or for reference.

CLARINET

| 00672423 | Buddy De Franco Collection | $19.95 |

FLUTE

00672379	Eric Dolphy Collection	$19.95
00672582	The Very Best of James Galway	$16.99
00672372	James Moody Collection – Sax and Flute	$19.95

GUITAR & BASS

00660113	The Guitar Style of George Benson	$14.95
00699072	Guitar Book of Pierre Bensusan	$29.95
00672331	Ron Carter – Acoustic Bass	$16.95
00672307	Stanley Clarke Collection	$19.95
00660115	Al Di Meola – Friday Night in San Francisco	$14.95
00604043	Al Di Meola – Music, Words, Pictures	$14.95
00672574	Al Di Meola – Pursuit of Radical Rhapsody	$22.99
00673245	Jazz Style of Tal Farlow	$19.95
00699306	Jim Hall – Exploring Jazz Guitar	$19.95
00604049	Allan Holdsworth – Reaching for the Uncommon Chord	$14.95
00699215	Leo Kottke – Eight Songs	$14.95
00675536	Wes Montgomery – Guitar Transcriptions	$17.95
00672353	Joe Pass Collection	$18.95
00673216	John Patitucci	$16.95
00027083	Django Reinhardt Antholog	$14.95
00026711	Genius of Django Reinhardt	$10.95
00672374	Johnny Smith Guitar Solos	$19.99

PIANO & KEYBOARD

00672338	Monty Alexander Collection	$19.95
00672487	Monty Alexander Plays Standards	$19.95
00672520	Count Basie Collection	$19.95
00672439	Cyrus Chestnut Collection	$19.95
00672300	Chick Corea – Paint the World	$12.95
14037739	Storyville Presents Duke Ellington	$19.99
00672537	Bill Evans at Town Hall	$16.95
00672548	The Mastery of Bill Evans	$12.95
00672425	Bill Evans – Piano Interpretations	$19.95
00672365	Bill Evans – Piano Standards	$19.95
00672510	Bill Evans Trio – Vol. 1: 1959-1961	$24.95
00672511	Bill Evans Trio – Vol. 2: 1962-1965	$24.95
00672512	Bill Evans Trio – Vol. 3: 1968-1974	$24.95
00672513	Bill Evans Trio – Vol. 4: 1979-1980	$24.95
00672381	Tommy Flanagan Collection	$24.99
00672492	Benny Goodman Collection	$16.95
00672486	Vince Guaraldi Collection	$19.95
00672419	Herbie Hancock Collection	$19.95
00672438	Hampton Hawes	$19.95
14037738	Storyville Presents Earl Hines	$19.99
00672322	Ahmad Jamal Collection	$22.95
00672564	Best of Jeff Lorber	$17.99
00672476	Brad Mehldau Collection	$19.99
00672388	Best of Thelonious Monk	$19.95
00672389	Thelonious Monk Collection	$19.95

00672390	Thelonious Monk Plays Jazz Standards – Volume 1	$19.95
00672391	Thelonious Monk Plays Jazz Standards – Volume 2	$19.95
00672433	Jelly Roll Morton – The Piano Rolls	$12.95
00672553	Charlie Parker for Piano	$19.95
00672542	Oscar Peterson – Jazz Piano Solos	$16.95
00672562	Oscar Peterson – A Jazz Portrait of Frank Sinatra	$19.95
00672544	Oscar Peterson – Originals	$9.95
00672532	Oscar Peterson – Plays Broadway	$19.95
00672531	Oscar Peterson – Plays Duke Ellington	$19.95
00672563	Oscar Peterson – A Royal Wedding Suite	$19.99
00672533	Oscar Peterson – Trios	$24.95
00672543	Oscar Peterson Trio – Canadiana Suite	$10.99
00672534	Very Best of Oscar Peterson	$22.95
00672371	Bud Powell Classics	$19.95
00672376	Bud Powell Collection	$19.95
00672507	Gonzalo Rubalcaba Collection	$19.95
00672303	Horace Silver Collection	$19.95
00672316	Art Tatum Collection	$22.95
00672355	Art Tatum Solo Book	$19.95
00672357	Billy Taylor Collection	$24.95
00673215	McCoy Tyner	$16.95
00672321	Cedar Walton Collection	$19.95
00672519	Kenny Werner Collection	$19.95
00672434	Teddy Wilson Collection	$19.95
14037740	Storyville Presents Teddy Wilson	$19.99

SAXOPHONE

00672566	The Mindi Abair Collection	$14.99
00673244	Julian "Cannonball" Adderley Collection	$19.95
00673237	Michael Brecker	$19.95
00672429	Michael Brecker Collection	$19.95
00672315	Benny Carter Plays Standards	$22.95
00672394	James Carter Collection	$19.95
00672349	John Coltrane Plays Giant Steps	$19.95
00672529	John Coltrane – Giant Steps	$14.99
00672494	John Coltrane – A Love Supreme	$14.95
00307393	John Coltrane – Omnibook: C Instruments	$24.99
00307391	John Coltrane – Omnibook: B-flat Instruments	$19.99
00307392	John Coltrane – Omnibook: E-flat Instruments	$24.99
00307394	John Coltrane – Omnibook: Bass Clef Instruments	$24.99
00672493	John Coltrane Plays "Coltrane Changes"	$19.95
00672453	John Coltrane Plays Standards	$19.95
00673233	John Coltrane Solos	$22.95
00672328	Paul Desmond Collection	$19.95
00672379	Eric Dolphy Collection	$19.95
00672530	Kenny Garrett Collection	$19.95
00699375	Stan Getz	$19.95

00672377	Stan Getz – Bossa Novas	$19.95
00672375	Stan Getz – Standards	$18.95
00673254	Great Tenor Sax Solos	$18.95
00672523	Coleman Hawkins Collection	$19.95
00673252	Joe Henderson – Selections from "Lush Life" & "So Near So Far"	$19.95
00672330	Best of Joe Henderson	$22.95
00672350	Tenor Saxophone Standards	$18.95
00673239	Best of Kenny G	$19.95
00673229	Kenny G – Breathless	$19.95
00672462	Kenny G – Classics in the Key of G	$19.95
00672485	Kenny G – Faith: A Holiday Album	$14.95
00672373	Kenny G – The Moment	$19.95
00672326	Joe Lovano Collection	$19.95
00672498	Jackie McLean Collection	$19.95
00672372	James Moody Collection – Sax and Flute	$19.95
00672416	Frank Morgan Collection	$19.95
00672539	Gerry Mulligan Collection	$19.95
00672352	Charlie Parker Collection	$19.95
00672561	Best of Sonny Rollins	$19.95
00672444	Sonny Rollins Collection	$19.95
00102751	Sonny Rollins with the Modern Jazz Quartet	$17.99
00675000	David Sanborn Collection	$17.95
00672528	Bud Shank Collection	$19.95
00672491	New Best of Wayne Shorter	$19.95
00672550	The Sonny Stitt Collection	$19.95
00672350	Tenor Saxophone Standards	$18.95
00672567	The Best of Kim Waters	$17.99
00672524	Lester Young Collection	$19.95

TROMBONE

| 00672332 | J.J. Johnson Collection | $19.95 |
| 00672489 | Steve Turré Collection | $19.99 |

TRUMPET

00672557	Herb Alpert Collection	$14.99
00672480	Louis Armstrong Collection	$17.95
00672481	Louis Armstrong Plays Standards	$17.95
00672435	Chet Baker Collection	$19.95
00672556	Best of Chris Botti	$19.95
00672448	Miles Davis – Originals, Vol. 1	$19.95
00672451	Miles Davis – Originals, Vol. 2	$19.95
00672450	Miles Davis – Standards, Vol. 1	$19.95
00672449	Miles Davis – Standards, Vol. 2	$19.95
00672479	Dizzy Gillespie Collection	$19.95
00673214	Freddie Hubbard	$14.95
00672382	Tom Harrell – Jazz Trumpet	$19.95
00672363	Jazz Trumpet Solos	$9.95
00672506	Chuck Mangione Collection	$19.95
00672525	Arturo Sandoval – Trumpet Evolution	$19.95

HAL•LEONARD CORPORATION

7777 W. BLUEMOUND RD. P.O. BOX 13819 MILWAUKEE, WI 53213

Visit our web site for a complete listing of our titles with songlists at

www.halleonard.com

0913